CAREERS IN

FORESTRY

ARE YOU GOOD AT SCIENCE? DO YOU have a passion for the great outdoors and a deep-rooted desire to protect the environment? Then consider a career in forestry. Surrounded by wildlife and lush woodlands, you will use your skills and knowledge to serve humanity and preserve the wilderness for generations to come.

Forestry offers jobs on the local, state, and national level, with employment opportunities in foreign countries as well. From forest rangers, to resource recreation managers, to urban foresters, this is a field with a wide range of careers. Foresters employ the latest advances in science and technology to address the numerous challenges and threats to the productive use of timberlands, without destroying this valuable natural resource.

Forestry is a career that encourages discovery and innovation. Imagine having a job developing methods to use wood more efficiently, or finding new, effective, expedient ways to battle forest fires, sparing more of this valuable land from needless ruin.

The view of forests has changed a great deal since early settlers came to North America. Heavily wooded areas were once considered a hindrance to progress. Forests were ravaged so farms and homesteads could be developed. However, as society gained knowledge of the important roles these bountiful lands play in the course of human survival, people started treating forests with greater respect, though it took centuries for these concepts to take hold.

Until just over one hundred years ago, forests were still being cut down without care or concern. Vast forests that provided so much humankind needed were being neglected. No attention was given to preventing disease, insects, soil erosion, and even fires, from destroying large swaths of forestland. There was little public recognition of the importance woodlands play in providing refuge for wildlife, help with climate control, clean water and air, and a peaceful, unblemished retreat for people of all ages. In addition, we depend on wood for products, from paper to furniture.

Maintaining healthy forests requires hard work, strategic planning, and endless care. Fortunately, the forestland that is left can still be saved, and that vital job falls to foresters. Future foresters will continue this proud tradition, armed with modern technology and applying it to enhance the growth of woodlands around the globe.

It can take up to 250 years for nature to produce mature, harvestable trees to replace those cut down. The demand for this wood is simply too great for nature to provide what is needed. Scientists working in forestry have found ways to grow trees on managed property in one-fifth the time and with six times the volume. People get the wood they need from these controlled wood-growing environments, and natural forestland can be preserved in its undisturbed state.

WHAT YOU CAN DO NOW

MOST PEOPLE WHO CHOOSE FORESTRY AS a career discover that they have an interest in the work early in life. That is why so many who end up as foresters get involved in scouting and nature programs as youngsters. These activities are an excellent way to expand your knowledge about forests and the wilderness, and to get hands-on experience through camping, hiking, and mountain climbing, as well as other adventures in the outdoors. Through these organizations, you also meet other people – both your own age and adults – who share your interest and are fascinated by the wonders of nature.

These groups teach resourcefulness and survival skills, plus respect for our natural environment. They give you valuable insights into what a career in forestry might entail. You also cultivate your leadership abilities through programs like these.

There are many books and educational films about forestry, and it is worth taking the time to seek out these materials and study them closely. The more you learn about forestry and nature, the easier it will be for you to decide if you want to make this your life's work.

Get involved with community groups that focus on conservation and environmental projects, such as park and river cleanups. You will be making a valuable contribution to your community, while learning about important issues that you will be dealing with if you pursue a career in forestry.

Follow news stories about the environment, conservation, and woodlands preservation.

HISTORY OF THE CAREER

JUST IMAGINE A WORLD WITHOUT forests. That is not as far-fetched as you might think. Through the ages, forests have often been the backdrop for historic events, but people took these lush woodlands for granted, destroying them in the name of progress.

Some historians believe China saw its wood supply dwindle at an alarming rate as far back as five thousand years ago. Meeting the needs of a growing population was blamed for the scarcity, but no conservation efforts were ever undertaken or even considered.

There were severe wood shortages in both the Greek and Roman Empires, primarily due to the careless way woodlands were cleared. At the peak of those empires, as demand for wood grew for heating homes and varied industrial purposes, including construction, forests were decimated. No one did any planning when it came to cutting down the trees and no efforts were made at reforestation. The damage was irreversible, causing rampant soil degradation. The lack of trees and foliage, especially around riverbanks, led to flooding that wiped out entire villages and valuable farmland.

In the Middle Ages, Europeans began to realize that there was not an endless supply of wood, and they began to take steps to restrict the wholesale clearing of some forestland. It was almost too late. Wood shortages started to affect industries in England, and slow shipbuilding in France. Some of the forestland was protected by the nobility – not to preserve timber but rather to provide the aristocracy with a quiet, private place to hunt.

Sylva, which means woods or forest, became the title of the first book on forestry. The work was published in 1664. Also known by the title *A Discourse of Forest-Trees and the Propagation of Timber in His Majesty's Dominions*, the book was penned by well-known British writer and conservationist John Evelyn. The text urged landowners to plant trees and gave descriptions of a variety of trees, along with ways to care for them. It was considered a handbook for forest management and ideas contained in the book spread throughout Europe.

Europeans thought they had found a way to ease their wood crisis with the settling of the New World. Failing to learn the lessons of thoughtless forest destruction in the Old World, many settlers continued to destroy valuable woodland to make way for homes, farms, and towns in America. British and French merchants would take shiploads of timber back to their homelands from the American colonies, cutting trees down with no forest management plan in mind.

Some colonists saw how fast the timber was disappearing. They knew that it could take up to 4,000 trees to build a large British warship, and loggers from Great Britain were stripping the early American countryside bare. Pennsylvania founder William Penn fought to have a clause put in land contracts in the American colonies that required leaving one acre of wooded land for every five acres cleared. For his part, Benjamin Franklin, one of the nation's founding fathers, invented a stove in 1741 that burned wood economically in an attempt to conserve the forest as a valuable, renewable natural resource.

Meanwhile, at the beginning of the 19th century, forest management was rapidly becoming popular as a career in Europe, employing many of John Evelyn's principles. This was the start of forestry as a recognized profession, with England, Germany, France, and Scandinavia all involved in the effort. By 1825, forestry schools were opening their doors to students across Europe.

It would take longer for the science of forestry to make its way to the United States. Following the American Revolution, fights broke out between individual landowners, towns, and states over who owned the forestland. The federal government started buying up these lands and put them in the public domain, meaning they belonged to everyone. After a while, the federal government was overwhelmed with land and started giving it away to timber companies, railroads, homesteaders, and just about anyone who answered the call.

The land was being cleared at a rapid rate. Loggers wasted almost as many trees as they harvested, in the rush to cut them down. Finally in 1847, a congressman from Vermont, named George Perkins Marsh, began advancing the idea of conserving the woodlands, and he warned of the dire consequences of depleting the nation's natural resources. Author Henry David Thoreau pushed for conservation through his writing and by giving public speeches on the subject.

In 1876, the US Congress first showed a true understanding of the importance of the woodlands when it ordered a study of the American forestland. That study resulted in the establishment in 1881 of the Division of Forestry in the US Department of Agriculture. Some states followed suit, starting their own forestry boards or commissions.

Another decade would pass before the President of the United States would be given the power to set aside forest reserves. Some 40 million acres would receive that protection within the next six years (1891-1897). The land still lacked management by skilled foresters. Toward the very end of the 19th century, colleges started offering courses in forestry and opening schools devoted to the subject.

Forests – and all natural resources – found one of their biggest supporters in Theodore Roosevelt, who became President of the United States in September 1901, following the assassination of William McKinley. When Roosevelt took office, his good friend, Gifford Pinchot, a respected forester, was already heading the Division of Forestry. Pinchot had started the Society of American Foresters in 1900 to bring credibility to the forestry profession. With the aid of Roosevelt, Pinchot began to convince Americans of the wisdom of conserving natural resources.

The two championed the concept of managing woodlands so that the nation could meet its needs for wood, while still preserving forestland and developing an active, effective, and ongoing plan for reforestation. In 1905 the Division of Forestry, also known as the Bureau of Forestry, became the US Forest Service. The Forest Service was put in charge of all the nation's forest reserves.

While forest management and the work of foresters were ingrained in American culture since the days of Theodore Roosevelt, it got another boost during the 1960s. As a generation started to take a passionate interest in the environment, forestry as a profession went through a resurgence that it still enjoys today. The initiatives to keep the outdoors pristine, conserve woodlands and open space, and stop air and water pollution, all brought attention to what can be done to save the environment. Some of the most exciting jobs connected to those efforts can be found in forestry.

WHERE YOU WILL WORK

MOST FORESTERS DECIDE LONG BEFORE they graduate from college that they want to go to work in blue jeans and boots, rather than a business suit. Spending plenty of time surrounded by trees and wildlife is much more appealing to them than life behind a desk.

In the United States, foresters are responsible for managing over 700 million acres of woodlands and work for a variety of public- and private-sector employers. Federal agencies, along with state, county, and city governments, are the biggest employers of foresters in the United States. The National Park Service, the US

Forest Service, the Bureau of Land Management, the National Resources Conservation Service, the US Fish and Wildlife Service, and the Environmental Protection Agency are among the federal agencies that have foresters on staff. Foresters also work for state and urban forestry bureaus.

The Canadian government hires foresters, as do other countries that have timberlands within their borders. Jobs in international forestry are growing, as a wood crisis looms in parts of India and Africa, stemming from poor forest management.

There are job options for foresters in the private sector as well. Water companies that own watershed land hire foresters to manage the property. Foresters oversee any tree removal from the watershed, work to maximize the amount of water produced on the property, and oversee water-quality maintenance.

In industry, foresters work for companies that produce wood products and own timberland. Some of these private companies include sawmills, pulp mills, paper companies, and tree nurseries. While many foresters manage these properties, some do research, including finding ways for companies to use as much of a tree as possible, thereby reducing waste.

Nonprofit environmental and conservation organizations, such as the Nature Conservancy, employ foresters to manage land, conduct research, and advise the public about what can be done to protect and preserve forestland.

Some foresters become private consultants. They assist private landowners with conservation, utilization, and management issues on forest property. According to the Society of American Foresters, almost 60 percent of forestland in the United States is owned privately, either by an individual, a family, a company, or an organization. While many private forestry consultants are self-employed, large forestry consulting firms have been established throughout the United States and employ numerous foresters on their staff.

A number of foresters forsake the outdoor workplace, at least part of the time, for the classroom. Universities and colleges hire foresters to teach, but they also use the talents of these timberland experts for community outreach, conservation, and environmental programs. These programs educate the public about forests, their ecosystems, and the impact they have on everyday life.

Academics are encouraged to do research as well. Some of these foresters go back out in the field, or they might spend time in a laboratory. Foresters in academia are often involved in applied research. They are trying to find solutions to pressing problems facing timberlands today, such as the increased threat of fires.

THE WORK YOU WILL DO

ONE OF THE MOST APPEALING ASPECTS of working in forestry is the wide range of jobs. Whatever your interests, if you want to preserve the woodlands, there is a job for you in forestry.

Foresters have so much to offer. In addition to a solid background in silviculture, foresters come to their jobs with a wealth of knowledge in geology, botany, zoology, meteorology, and economics.

While different jobs in forestry may focus on different facets of the work, everyone in this profession is striving to reach the same goal – conserving and protecting the woodlands. With that in mind, foresters working on all levels have to deal with numerous regulations, ethical considerations, environmental issues, and conservation concerns. They have to strike the right balance in everything they do to safeguard this natural resource, while meeting the needs of business interests and recreational users.

There are certain tasks every forester is involved in. It will be part of your role to advocate for the woodlands to be used so their productivity, vitality, regeneration capacity, and biodiversity are not compromised. You are part scientist and part politician. As debates rage on about how forestland should be used, foresters are often plunged into the middle of the public discourse. Presenting the scientific facts is as important as rallying public support for doing what is best for the timberland.

Since forests are one of the greatest assets of a nation, foresters have to market woodlands as such. People have to be constantly reminded of all the good that can derived from a single forest.

Forest professionals often point out that a forest is much more valuable than an oil well. An oil well may eventually run dry, they argue. By contrast, carefully managed woodlands using reforestation techniques can continue to produce wood forever.

Forest Manager

Forest management is one of the prestige jobs in forestry, and this job carries a great deal of responsibility. Working on either public or privately owned forestland, each forest manager does just about everything that is needed on the land tract. The most important task is developing a master plan for how the land will be used.

Managers keep inventories of the woodlands they oversee. They know what kinds of trees and vegetation are on the land, how plentiful they are, and their general location on the tract. The whole ecosystem is in your purview. You study the local soil and geology. You also study the waterways, if any are located on the woodlands. As a forest manager, you record the various kinds of wildlife.

Inventories cover the ages and size of the tree population – anything that might be unique to the forestland is catalogued. This information all plays a vital role in the wide-ranging decisions the manager has to make when it comes to land use.

Appraisals of harvestable trees must be made, and the forest manager is in charge of doing that or having it done. Using that data, you can develop a plan for harvesting trees. That plan includes a timetable for the harvest, a plan for how the harvest will be done to create the least possible upheaval in the rest of the woodlands, and reforestation.

Once the harvest begins, even though there might be a foreman on the job, it is ultimately the responsibility of the forest manager to direct the logging effort. Inspecting the trees for disease and insect infestation, and having a method ready for preventing this kind of blight, are important duties.

The manager has to be knowledgeable about how climate might impact the forest, including potential damage from heavy rain and winds. A plan to prevent forest fires falls to the timberland manager, as does the job of restoration if a forest fire does strike.

While there are many regulations to protect and preserve both public and private timberland, it is up to forest managers and their team to enforce those regulations. They have to ensure that members of the public using the forest abide by all the rules and restrictions.

Foresters who manage private forests owned by timber companies, sawmills, pulp mills, tree nurseries, and other commercial enterprises, have to see that no shortcuts are taken when trees are harvested, no needless destruction is caused to the land during the harvest, and that the land is used to its maximum productivity, in addition to making certain all government laws are followed. When managing a privately owned forestland tract, the forest manager has the added burden of ensuring that conservation comes first, not profit.

Resource Recreation Manager

One of the fastest-growing segments of the forestry field is resource recreation management. Recreation plays a major role in how forestland is used.

Basically, this forester is in charge of facilitating people having fun. The resource recreation manager designs and implements hiking trails, campgrounds, picnic areas, bird-watching tours, berry-picking outings, nature treks, photography expeditions – anything that can be done for fun in nature's playground.

Procurement Forester

Some companies that rely heavily on wood do not have their own timberlands. To get the lumber they need, these companies hire a procurement forester. Many private citizens own forestland. If they are willing to sell some of their trees, companies can buy timber from these individuals. The harvest must comply with all government laws regarding the removal of trees from forestland. That is where the procurement forester comes in.

These experts appraise the trees, negotiate a price, and, most importantly, develop a plan for harvesting and reforestation. Once the deal is made, the procurement forester hires a contractor to do the harvest and oversees the work to make sure it is done properly.

Procurement foresters are usually private consultants. A group of companies frequently get together to share the expenses to obtain the timber they need. The companies hire the same procurement forester to buy timber for all of them. The wood is then divided among the consortium.

Urban Forester

Urban foresters do their job surrounded by concrete. Working in heavily populated areas, like cities and towns, urban foresters manage the trees and greenery that take root in these municipal settings. The job of an urban forester is much different from that of foresters who work in wilderness woodlands, surrounded by wide--open spaces.

Urban foresters plan parks, as well as landscapes, in neighborhoods and along busy highways. They deal with problems rarely seen in wilderness forests and open timberland, like power lines threatening the limbs of trees that bring shade to hot city streets. Ecosystems in cities are complex and present different problems than the ones in a traditional forest, including assessing the effects of daily exposure to noxious fumes on natural life. Some trees have stood in cities for centuries and are considered neighborhood treasures. Urban foresters work to preserve them, keeping them safe from disease and the other perils to nature that lurk in the city.

Forest Scientist

As the world population grows, it continues to put a strain on wood supplies. Forest scientists find ways to grow trees faster and with the traits needed for specific uses. These foresters specialize in biotechnology and tree genetics. Their research unearths ways to grow trees that are resistant to destructive insects and that will not fall victim to disease.

New methods to prevent forest fires come from the research done by forest scientists, as do cutting-edge techniques to fight fires in timberlands, and limit loss from fires. These foresters work to gain a better understanding of forest ecosystems and invent new approaches to wood processing.

Forest Engineers

While forest managers formulate harvesting plans, many rely on proven methods perfected by forest engineers. These engineers come up with these methods based on conditions found in forests all over the world.

Foresters who make engineering their specialty are often called on to design new and more efficient equipment to harvest timber. They develop forward-thinking ideas on how to build roadways inside woodlands to get loggers and their equipment to and from harvest areas. Forest engineers often plan roads that can be returned to their natural state after the project is completed.

Sometimes a harvesting effort will necessitate building permanent culverts, bridges, or drains. A forest engineer designs this infrastructure.

There are even occasions when a new forest will be laid out in an attempt to create woodlands in what was once wide-open acreage. A forest engineer is called in to design this new timberland so it is most conducive to producing as many trees as possible to meet the demand for wood.

Forestry Technician

Forestry technicians have one of the most diverse and demanding jobs in the timberlands. These foresters work under the supervision of forest managers. They are experts at identifying the plant life, wildlife, and trees in a forest.

Forest technicians get their hands dirty. They plant new trees, control soil erosion, care for trees, work on stream enhancement, help maintain recreation areas and the woodlands in general, do inspections, check property boundaries, and handle a myriad of other jobs, including supervising seasonal workers.

Forest Rangers

With millions of acres of forestland in the United States, forest rangers are on the front lines in the battle to protect the woodlands and those who use them. Considered foresters as well, these men and women are dedicated to forest conservation and preservation, and are also first responders in case of an emergency.

Forest rangers patrol the forestland on foot, on horseback, on skis or snowshoes, in planes, and in cars. Part of their job is to enforce the law in forests throughout the nation, but they also work as tour guides and educators; maintain roads, trails, and buildings in the woodlands; and monitor wildlife and plant species throughout the property. The day-in-day-out patrols made by these rangers help identify careless practices by campers, hikers, and others in the forest, and help prevent accidents and forest fires.

Forest-Products Industry

More than five thousand different products are made from wood. Wood by-products turn up in everything from feedstock to plastic. So it is not surprising that many foresters find employment in the forest-products industry. Foresters can use their talents to help develop new products made from wood.

People have always depended on wood and, since wood is a renewable resource, unlike metal, foresters are always working on finding new ways to use timber. Foresters working in the wood--products industry strive to make wood-processing operations more energy efficient. Research is also going on in the paper and pulp industry, since half the trees harvested are turned into paper.

There is money to be made in these innovations. When new products are discovered, foresters are often the best people to market them. Who better to market a wood derivative than someone who really understands where it comes from and how it is made?

STORIES OF FORESTRY PROFESSIONALS

I Am an Urban Forester

"I became an urban forester because I believe the trees and plants that make up ecosystems in cities throughout the world are neglected and often taken for granted. This greenery is really the only connection people living in an urban area have to nature, and it's my job to preserve it and keep it vibrant.

I am fortunate enough to work in a city that has many parks, and the trees, plants, shrubs, grasses, and soil in those areas are my responsibility. Yes, there are those days I would rather be working in a traditional forest out in the middle of nowhere. People understand what the forester's job is all about in that kind of setting. In a city, taxpayers don't always realize why a forester is on the payroll.

My job is very important from a number of standpoints. Vegetation in urban areas – especially trees – reduces storm water runoff, improves air quality, cuts down on soil erosion, beautifies neighborhoods, and increases property values.

We can't afford to lose a single tree. But there are times when trees are decayed and dying, and it's my job to evaluate those trees – whether they're on a city street or in a park – and make a decision about whether that tree has to be cut down. I also recommend replanting trees in those areas, and I make sure the right kind of tree is planted and that the ground is prepared properly (the right soil, deep enough hole) to plant that kind of tree. If a city does not cut down decaying trees, there is a real risk that the tree, or a large branch, might come down during a rain or windstorm and injure somebody or destroy a house.

I also make sure that if branches from a tree have to be trimmed, because they interfere with power lines, the work is done properly so the tree is not damaged and can still thrive. I work with the city's Department of Public Works to figure out ways to repair sidewalks when a tree root has grown so big it begins to buckle the pavement.

Trees can be damaged in car accidents and fall prey to vandals. It is part of my job to evaluate those trees and see what can be done to save or, if necessary, restore them.

I have an inventory of all the trees in the city. I make sure the trees are free of disease and insect infestation, which, when left untreated, can weaken or kill a tree and create a safety hazard, not to mention spreading to other trees.

When there is any construction in the city, if there are trees or shrubs on the job site, I go down and find ways for the work to be done without killing or removing the greenery. I serve as an advocate for keeping foliage in the city. I organize volunteers to help plant trees and shrubs in some areas that need them, so city dwellers get involved in urban beautification.

Working in an urban setting, rather than a wilderness, you learn how precious each tree and shrub is."

I Am a Forest Manager

"Being a forest manager is like being the mayor of a small city. The difference, of course, is my constituents are trees, plants, and wildlife. My job is to provide services and protect their best interests.

Like running a city, major issues come up all the time, and my decisions impact my constituents and what happens on the land for generations to come. I deal with everything any municipal elected official does, including law enforcement, new development, health issues, economic considerations, environmental impact, infrastructure, working with government agencies, and protecting natural resources.

What is interesting about this job is you know going in that you need exceptional science skills, but you also must have administrative skills. You have to be extremely well organized and have an eye for hiring good people so you can delegate responsibility.

This can be a complex job. Everybody views the forest in a different way. Some see it in a commercial vein – the economics of harvesting timber. Others view it from strictly a recreational standpoint. Everybody who approaches you with a concern about the forest is passionate about it, but the bottom line for me has to be what is best for the woodlands.

I don't think anyone gets into this field for any reason other than to protect the forestland. I think all foresters are aware of all the forestland that has been destroyed through the ages. While many people believe there is plenty of forestland left, foresters view it as a dwindling natural resource that can begin to vanish with the wrong public policy. That is why we are all advocates for the preservation of forests.

One of our greatest weapons in this battle is education. We want people – especially young people – to realize the importance of forests and what they mean to our planet. Hopefully, along the way, we encourage some youngsters to become foresters, but at least we hope to get them to take a lifelong interest in forest preservation.

This career calls for a deep understanding of how everything in the forest interacts within its ecosystem. You have to be able to identify trees, plants, and wildlife on sight. Your education doesn't end when you get out of college – on this job it never ends. I can't remember a day that has gone by when I didn't learn something new. The forest is a great teacher.

Of course, I didn't start out as a forest manager. I worked for a number of years as a forestry technician and worked my way up. You need a good education to get into this field, but you learn a great deal once you are on the job.

I think one thing that people have to realize if they want to become foresters is that this is a physically demanding job. You have to be in shape when you start out in this job and stay in shape your whole career. This is a job where you constantly exercise your mind and your body."

I Am a Forestry Technician

"I was never one to sit behind a desk, and I never wanted to be bored at work. I don't have those problems on this job.

I wasn't quite sure why so many people who go into forestry started out as forestry technicians, but now I see why. You come across everything in this job and it really prepares you to move up to a management position. You can do that if you have a bachelor's or a graduate degree in this field. Many people work as forestry technicians while studying for a master's degree.

This is a very hands-on job, and you do a bit of everything, including handling and using heavy equipment. There is a great deal of inventory work and record keeping. We measure trees for height and diameter. Once we have that information, we can figure out how much lumber a particular tree can yield. That's important when it comes to deciding which trees to harvest.

Just to give you an idea of how varied the work of a forestry technician is from day to day, here are some of the assignments I've had:

Maintaining and marking trails
Pruning trees
Removing dead trees
Planting, mulching, and watering trees
Clearing out heavy underbrush
Selecting trees for harvest
Inspecting trees for insects and dead branches
Standing watch for fires in the lookout tower
Checking the forest after visitors have left to make sure all campfires have been put out
Maintaining recreation areas
Aiding injured campers and hikers

I often work in remote areas of the forest. Sometimes I have to hike to a work site with a backpack filled with heavy equipment. Other times I can use an all-terrain vehicle, but it's rarely an easy ride.

I think you have to have a sense of adventure to do this job. The terrain can be rough and rocky, the inclines steep. There is always the risk of injury, no matter how careful you are, from stings, bites, and even falling tree limbs. We train to avoid these injuries. You have to always be alert on this job and expect the unexpected. Safety is paramount.

There are many days I work alone in the woods, so you have to be comfortable with that. You work out in the forest in all kinds of weather. Bad weather conditions don't mean a day off! Hot, humid, steamy days can make working in the forest pretty tough, especially when you are wearing protective clothing and gear, and lugging heavy equipment around. You get dirty in this job, but you accomplish something every day."

PERSONAL QUALIFICATIONS

A STRONG BACKGROUND IN SCIENCE IS A MUST for anyone going into a forestry career.

Topping the list of personal qualities are people skills. As a forester, you will be working with many people, from campers and hikers to government officials and corporate executives. You have to be able to establish a working relationship with each of them. You have to understand their goals and concerns, and be able to address a variety of issues.

That makes you a problem solver. You will often be confronted with an issue that has two sides arguing with each other. In those types of situations, what is best for the forestland is frequently overlooked. You have to remind people that the forest is for everyone and make suggestions that will speak to all the concerns that have been voiced. You might feel like more of a diplomat at times.

Foresters have to be energetic. You will find yourself on the go much of the time. Whether you are hiking to a far-off part of the forest to complete a tree inventory, or speaking before a civic group about the importance of forests to the environment, foresters have very little downtime during the course of the day.

Foresters work with many different professionals who share the same goals and objectives, making teamwork vital to success. You will cross paths with silviculturists, wildlife scientists, entomologists, and others working to preserve and protect forests. They will be as passionate about the mission as you are. Being comfortable working with a team of experts and playing your role as part of that team will be necessary.

Whether you are managing recreation areas or logging areas, being a forester requires creative planning skills. You have to be able to come up with a master plan for the forest you oversee and be able to clearly explain the wisdom of that plan.

You might come up with a new way to approach an old problem, or find a solution to a nagging issue. To do that, you have to pay attention to detail as you develop a plan that addresses all the concerns and issues raised. There is research required to see what has been tried, what has worked, and what has not and why.

To present your plan, you need good communications skills – both speaking and writing. You may have to write a report outlining your plan. You might then have to defend that plan at a series of public meetings, with government officials and members of the public asking you questions.

ATTRACTIVE FEATURES

DECIDING TO PURSUE FORESTRY IS much more than a career choice – it is a commitment to making the world a better place.

Forests play a critical role in the environment, sustaining wildlife and providing recreational activities for people who crave the serene surroundings of beautiful forests. So your work has a meaningful impact day after day, season after season.

As you walk through the clean, plentiful forestland where you work, you can take pride in all you see around you and the ongoing work you do to keep the land that way. While many people talk about preserving the environment, you are actually doing it.

You are learning something new on the job all the time. There is always a piece of the forest in your life. The work never gets boring. Different issues come up all the time and you have the opportunity to find innovative ways to solve these problems and to set the agenda for addressing timberland concerns for years to come.

Saving natural resources inspires you to do your best every day, and you get to see and study these extraordinary wonders firsthand. This is a job where you are encouraged to explore your surroundings. Getting close to wildlife that many people only see on TV is an everyday occurrence. All forms of plant life flourish as a result of your daily efforts.

Taking what you learn and witness on your job, you educate others about what is needed to keep woodlands vibrant, productive, and useful. You are a liaison between the forest and the public, letting people know how prominently these vast wooded habitats figure in their lives and what everyone can do to help keep them healthy.

Forestry work helps keep you in shape. Some days you might have to backpack, hiking a winding trail to get to an area you have to inspect, one that many people never get the opportunity to see. Other days you might travel on horseback to get to your work site, and that sure beats sitting in city traffic to get to a stuffy office.

There is always a possibility that you will see something you have never seen before when you work in forestry. Throughout the world, there are over fifty thousand different species of trees. Every region has different ones, every forest you work in or visit can reveal something you have never seen before, and can broaden your on-the-job experience.

Throughout history, forests have been callously exploited by "cut-and-run" loggers who have no regard for the nature they destroy. They never replant the trees they cut down and give no thought to the wildlife they displace and the waterways they disrupt. Foresters have the satisfaction of serving as the first line of defense against these plunderers.

UNATTRACTIVE FEATURES

FORESTRY IS AN EXTREMELY CHALLENGING career, both intellectually and physically. Foresters on all levels must come up with ways to meet the needs of everyone who utilizes, enjoys, and benefits from the woodlands without showing favoritism to one forest patron over another. For example, you might be asked to develop a plan to remove timber from a forest, while still preserving its hiking trials, waterways, natural beauty, and wildlife refuge areas. You have to maintain a delicate balance to protect everyone's interests.

Managing forestland is similar to running a small city or town – your decisions will be both cheered and jeered. Try as you might, you will not please everyone. Working to convince those who love the forest, but disagree with your vision for it, and getting them to give your plans a chance, can be both stressful and frustrating. So can making the public understand that forests serve multiple purposes and, when managed properly, are an infinite resource.

Logging need not destroy the solitude of a wooded retreat. Trees can be cut down in one area of the forest and then replanted, while wildlife, plants, and activities in other parts of the habitat are unaffected. Still, you will have your opponents and, though your methods may be generally accepted, persuading those who oppose your approach can be time consuming and frustrating, and can take you away from other pressing issues.

In the early years of their careers, many foresters work outdoors. This is physically demanding and exhausting work. In addition, the job has to be done regardless of weather conditions, including rain, snow, and high winds. In fact, this may be when you are needed the most.

You go where the forest is located. Some of these woodlands are in remote areas, so landing a job close to home may not always be possible. Housing in these remote areas may be difficult to find and, if living in the forest is required, you might have to forgo some modern-day amenities and comforts.

Seeing the forest abused in any way can be heartbreaking. This is especially true when uncaring people break forest rules, or carelessness leads to one of the worst catastrophes that can happen in these timberlands – fire. Having to watch as fire, and the destruction it wreaks, spread through wooded landscapes can be agonizing. Walking through the affected areas after a fire is one of the most difficult tasks you have to face on this job.

EDUCATION AND TRAINING

THERE ARE MANY WELL-RESPECTED forestry programs offered in colleges throughout the United States. Forestry is a very popular course of study as more young people are looking for green jobs.

It is important to take a close look at these programs before applying to a college because each is slightly different and may put more of an emphasis on a specialized area that you would like to focus on. The Society of American Foresters accredits most college forestry programs.

The best jobs in the forestry field require at least a bachelor's degree, and many employers favor candidates with a master's degree.

The Forestry Department at Michigan State University (MSU) in East Lansing was started in 1902 and is the oldest ongoing forestry program in the United States. For a Bachelor of Science degree at

MSU, students study environmental sciences, ecology, biology, public policy, and economics, and how these all relate to forests. Master of Science and doctoral degrees are also offered through MSU's Forestry Department.

MSU has an excellent extension program and is a major supporter of the Christmas tree industry in Michigan. The university's forestry program also maintains an up-to-date placement service for graduating forestry students.

Michigan Technological University (MTU) in Houghton also has one of the oldest forestry programs. The school offers a variety of Bachelor of Science degrees in forestry and environmental sciences. Students can pursue a master's and a doctoral degree in forestry at MTU as well.

MTU's course of study is enhanced by the school's 4,500-acre teaching forest, located 40 miles from campus. Ford Forest is used by MTU students as a natural outdoor laboratory. The forest is one of only a few teaching forests.

The School of Forestry and Wildlife Sciences at Auburn University in Alabama is renowned for its forestry curriculum. Courses include forest tree physiology, wood sciences and products, forest health, forest economics, and forest management. The school also teaches forest engineering. Graduate degrees in forestry are also available at Auburn. The college is known for its independent research in a number of areas of forestry, ecology, and wood products.

Oregon State University (OSU) College of Forestry in Corvallis has undergraduate programs in forest engineering, forestry management, natural resources, recreation resource management, tourism and outdoor leadership, and renewable materials. Students who are planning to attend OSU College of Forestry are urged to take advanced courses in biology, chemistry, and physics in high school. Graduate degrees are also offered at OSU. The university prides itself on its connections with a number of state and federal agencies, including the Bureau of Land Management and the US Forest Service, to help students find jobs upon graduation.

An intensive, three-week field course, offered every other year at the Kemp Natural Resources Station in Woodruff, Wisconsin, is part of the forestry program at the University of Wisconsin-Madison's Department of Forest and Wildlife Ecology. The school boasts a very active forestry club, primarily made up of undergraduate forestry majors. The forest science undergraduate program encompasses courses in conservation, economics, biology, forest ecology, and forest management. Wildlife and fishery, forest and the environment, and ecology are also among the courses of study at the university. Graduate studies can be pursued in areas from silvaculture and tree physiology, to forest and environmental policy.

The forest resources and conservation major in the School of Forest Resources and Conservation at the University of Florida in Gainesville requires courses in forest ecology, tree biology, soil science, and resource inventory, plus an array of other courses. The program teaches students how to manage ecosystems and gives them a solid understanding of ecology. A graduate program includes both a master's and a doctorate in forest resources and conservation. Urban forestry, international forestry, forest genetics, fire science, and tropical forestry are some of the courses studied by graduate students.

The College of Agricultural Sciences at Penn State University in University Park features an excellent Forest Science Research Center, where work is going on in biotechnology, forest genetics, natural regeneration, sustainable forestry, and forest management and planning. Students can choose from a variety of forestry options, including watershed management, urban forestry, forest management, and forest biology. Graduate studies range from forest resources and soil science, to wildlife and fisheries science.

Among other universities with outstanding forestry programs are the University of Minnesota in Minneapolis, Warner College of Natural Resources at Colorado State University in Fort Collins, West Virginia University in Morgantown, University of Alaska in Fairbanks, Purdue University in Indiana, and Mississippi State University.

A number of technical colleges, community colleges, junior colleges, and some four-year schools (such as Michigan Technological University) offer two-year associate degrees in forestry technology. These include Green River Community College in Auburn, Washington; Eastern Oklahoma State College in Wilburton; Abraham Baldwin Agricultural College in Tifton, Georgia; and Horry-Georgetown Technical College in Georgetown, South Carolina.

Educational requirements for forest rangers vary, depending on the particular government agency and whether you are applying for a job on the federal or state level. Some agencies only require a high school diploma, though most want an associate or bachelor's degree in forestry, ecology, forest management, or a related field.

Upon meeting certain criteria, which include at least a bachelor's degree, the Society of American Foresters (SAF) certifies foresters. Though not mandatory to work in the field, SAF certification is an impressive credential to have. To obtain SAF certification, you must have at least five years of professional experience and pass a comprehensive exam.

Some states, including California, Michigan, and Massachusetts, have made it mandatory for foresters to be either state-licensed or registered to practice. The licensing/registration process is conducted by a state forestry board. The requirements vary from state to state but usually have both an educational and an on-the-job-experience component.

EARNINGS

BECAUSE FORESTRY OFFERS A WIDE range of jobs, salaries vary as well. A determining factor when it comes to earnings is your level of education and experience. People with graduate degrees find more jobs in management and earn higher salaries. Hands-on experience helps you both land a job and advance in this field. A heavy emphasis is placed on internships.

Forestry jobs in private industry pay more than similar jobs in the public sector. Forest managers working for private companies earn between $85,000 and $125,000 a year, while forest managers employed by a government agency take home between $75,000 and $100,000. Urban foresters enjoy the same pay range, though most of them tend to find jobs in government.

Procurement foresters work mostly in the private sector and earn between $70,000 and $90,000. However, many procurement foresters do not tie themselves down to one company, and instead work as private consultants to many companies.

Forest engineers and forest scientists are the highest earners in this field, with salaries between $150,000 and $200,000 in the private sector, and $130,000 and $150,000 in government work. Forest scientists find many of their jobs in the forest products industry, doing research and finding innovative ways to use wood in everyday life. Other foresters working in sales and marketing in the forest products industry can earn between $85,000 and $100,000 annually.

Forest technicians and forest rangers have similar pay scales. The job pays $35,000 to $55,000 in the private sector, and $25,000 to $50,000 on the government payroll.

OPPORTUNITIES

THERE WILL BE JOB GROWTH IN THE forestry field over the next decade. Many of those jobs will be in the public sector – in federal, state, and local government agencies. Several developments are being credited for this increase in government forestry jobs. There has been an alarming number of devastating and costly forest fires in recent years. Foresters play a crucial role in finding ways not only to prevent these fires but to fight fires more effectively and to limit damage from them.

After a fire, foresters are assigned the difficult task of breathing new life into these scorched lands, and discovering ways to restore them to their former health. Recovery after a severe forest fire is a government priority these days, and that will mean growth in the forestry profession.

Government officials on all levels, especially the federal level, are pledging more money for forest fire prevention, as well as to better control and battle these blazes when they do happen. Part of this process involves having foresters on site during these infernos, learning as much as they can about what causes these fires. These forest professionals also learn how to best contain fires.

Wood is the focus of a great deal of attention as a renewable source of energy. So foresters with this kind of expertise will find an increasing number of jobs in government agencies dealing with energy in the coming years.

Urban forestry has taken on greater importance as green areas continue to shrink in city settings. City dwellers have developed a new appreciation for these reprieves from concrete, so maintaining these rare green areas amid tall buildings will present job opportunities for an increasing number of foresters.

There will also be growth in private-sector forestry jobs in the timber, logging, and wood-products industries. More foresters will be needed to manage private timberlands. They are ultimately responsible for making sure workers at sawmills, pulp factories, and other private companies operating in the woodlands abide by government regulations to protect the forest. As government ramps up enforcement of these laws, foresters will play an even greater role in these private companies.

Nonprofit environmental organizations concerned with forest preservation and replanting, as well as conservation, are expected to increase the size of their staffs. Their ongoing efforts include making sure governments in countries around the world are doing everything possible to protect forestland, including leaving some of it completely untouched, in a natural wilderness state.

Experienced foresters are needed in the classroom. A greater demand for forest professionals requires more people to teach them about the field and its enormous challenges.

GETTING STARTED

YOU NEED TO DO SOME RESEARCH AND make some decisions about your career before you finish college and enter the job market.

First, you have to decide if you want to work in the public or private sector. This decision comes more easily if you complete internships while you are in college. Internships in forestry give you a chance to work in the field and apply some of the concepts you learned in the classroom.

Practically everyone who goes into forestry has to spend some time in the field after graduating from college. Getting experience is a must.

Several years before leaving college, you should study the forestry job market. Visit state and local agencies that hire foresters as well as federal agencies, if you can. Explore forests in your area, and speak with the people who work there to gain insight into employment in the forestry field.

Some colleges invite representatives from government forestry agencies to visit the campus and conduct interviews with students. It is advisable to attend as many of these sessions as possible. Listen and ask questions about how the agencies work, what job openings there are, and the opportunities for advancement.

If a particular government agency seems like a good fit, but you cannot arrange to see the operation firsthand and the agency does not send a representative to visit your college, contact officials at that agency and find out if there is a brochure, website, or articles you can read to learn more about the organization. The same holds true for a private company that you would like to work for but know little about.

The more you learn about prospective employers, the better equipped you are to make a decision about whether you would like to work there, especially on a long-term basis. Remember, you might have to relocate for some jobs, so you will want to research the community where you will be moving.

Keep up-to-date on all the issues facing forestry. Knowledge evolves in the field of forestry and government policy regarding forest conservation and preservation shifts in response. These issues are bound to come up during a job interview, and it is a good idea for you to have all the facts, and formulate your own views. Read forestry journals on a regular basis, and check the websites of forestry societies and environmental and conservation groups worldwide. Attend forestry conferences to make job contacts and meet people who have years of experience in forestry. You will gain perspective on what is driving the field.

ASSOCIATIONS

■ **Society of American Foresters (SAF)**
http://www.safnet.org

■ **American Forests**
http://www.americanforests.org

■ **American Forest and Paper Association**
http://www.afandpa.org

■ **American Wood Council (AWC)**
http://www.awc.org

■ **American Wood Protection Association (AWPA)**
http://www.awpa.com

■ **National Association of State Foresters (NASF)**
http://www.stateforesters.org

■ **The Association of Consulting Foresters of America (ACF)**
www.acf-foresters.org/default.aspx

■ **Society of Municipal Arborists (SMA)**
http://www.urban-forestry.com

■ **Council on Forest Engineering (COFE)**
http://cofe.org

PERIODICALS

■ **Journal of Forestry**

The Forestry Source

Forest Science

Northern Journal of Applied Science

Southern Journal of Applied Science

Western Journal of Applied Science

Forest Files

American Forests Magazine

Forest Products Journal

International Journal of Forest Engineering

Wood and Fiber Science

WEBSITES

■ **US Forest Service**
http://www.fs.fed.us

■ **National Parks Conservation Association (NPCA)**
http://www.npca.org

■ **The Nature Conservancy**
http://www.nature.org

■ **Canadian Forestry Association**
http://canadianforestry.com/wp/?lang=en

■ **National Forest Recreation Association (NFRA)**
http://nfra.org

■ **International Council of Forest & Paper Associations (ICFPA)**
http://www.icfpa.org

■ **Forest Products Society**
http://www.forestprod.org

■ **Southern Forest Products Association (SFPA)**
http://www.sfpa.org

■ **Northwest Forestry Association**
http://nwtrees.org

■ **Western Forestry and Conservation Association (WFCA)**
http://www.westernforestry.org

■ **Tree Care Industry Association (TCIA)**
http://tcia.org

■ **Society of Wood Science and Technology (SWST)**
http://www.swst.org

SCHOOLS

■ **Michigan State University**
http://www.for.msu.edu/about

■ **Michigan Technological University**
http://www.mtu.edu/forest

■ **Auburn University**
http://wp.auburn.edu/sfws

■ **Oregon State University**
www.forestry.oregonstate.edu

■ **University of Wisconsin-Madison**
http://forestandwildlifeecology.wisc.edu

■ **University of Florida**
http://sfrc.ufl.edu

■ **Penn State University**
http://ecosystems.psu.edu
/majors/forest-science

■ **University of Minnesota**
www.forestry.umn.edu

■ **Colorado State University**
http://warnercnr.colostate.edu

■ **West Virginia University**
http://forestry.wvu.edu

■ **University of Alaska**
www.uaf.edu/snre/about/departments/forestry

■ **Purdue University**
https://ag.purdue.edu/fnr/Pages/default.aspx

■ **Mississippi State University**
http://www.cfr.msstate.edu

■ **Green River Community College**
www.naturalresourceseducation.com

■ **Eastern Oklahoma State College**
http://www.eosc.edu/academics
/degree_programsagriculture
_division/agriculture_degrees/forest_technology.aspx

■ **Abraham Baldwin Agricultural College**
http://www.abac.edu/academics
/schools/ag-natural-resources/forest-resources

■ **Horry-Georgetown Technical College**
http://www.hgtc.edu/academics
/academic_departments
/Naturalresources_main.html